THE LIBRARY OF
AMERICAN
LIVES AND TIMES™

STEPHEN F. AUSTIN

and the Founding of Texas

James L. Haley

The Rosen Publishing Group's
PowerPlus Books™
New York

To My Mother,
Still Loving, Still Caring

Published in 2003 by The Rosen Publishing Group, Inc.
29 East 21st Street, New York, NY 10010

First Edition

Editor's Note: All quotations have been reproduced as they appeared in the letters and diaries from which they were borrowed. No correction was made to the inconsistent spelling that was common in that time period.

Library of Congress Cataloging-in-Publication Data

Haley, James L.
Stephen F. Austin and the founding of Texas / James L. Haley.—1st ed.
p. cm. — (Library of American lives and times)
Includes bibliographical references (p.) and index.
Summary: Surveys the life of Stephen Austin, an American pioneer, who later became one of the founders of Texas.
  ISBN 0-8239-5738-1 (library binding)
1. Austin, Stephen F. (Stephen Fuller), 1793–1836—Juvenile literature.
2. Pioneers—Texas—Biography—Juvenile literature. 3. Texas—History—Revolution, 1835–1836—Juvenile literature. 4. Texas—History—To 1846—Juvenile literature. 5. Frontier and pioneer life—Texas—Juvenile literature. [1. Austin, Stephen F. (Stephen Fuller), 1793–1836. 2. Pioneers. 3. Texas—History—To 1846.]   I. Title. II. Series.
  F389.A942 H35 2003
  976.4'03—dc21

                                        2001004955

Manufactured in the United States of America

CONTENTS

1. Driven Father, Tormented Son

In the early years of the United States's independence, most people lived along the Atlantic Coast, on the same lands that had been the thirteen British colonies. The western frontier had hardly moved west of the Appalachian Mountains. The unsettled lands beyond, though, were seen as an opportunity for men who were hungry to make a fortune. Many men who had failed in business near their homes, or who were willing to gamble that they could make more of themselves on new land, were drawn to the edge of the wilderness. One such man was Moses Austin, a native of Durham, Connecticut.

Moses Austin was born in 1761, the son of an innkeeper who was also a tailor and farmer. These were humble occupations that did not suit Moses's higher ambitions. At the age of twenty-two he left home and moved to Philadelphia, Pennsylvania. There he went into business with his brother, Stephen, as a dry goods merchant. Two

---

Opposite: This is a map of North America as it appeared in 1784. The land was divided into territories belonging to Britain and Spain.

This portrait is believed to be of Moses Austin. It is the only known likeness that exists today of Stephen F. Austin's father. Moses Austin was the first man to obtain permission to bring Anglo-American settlers into Spanish Texas.

years later, in 1785, he found a shorter path to wealth when he married Mary Brown, whose father had made a fortune in real estate and iron mining. The young couple then moved to Richmond, Virginia, where Austin opened a branch of his dry goods store, and they quickly prospered. They moved into one of the largest houses in the city and owned several slaves. They also tried to start a family, but both of their little girls died in infancy.

Still looking to do better for himself, Moses Austin received a contract to build a lead roof over the Virginia capitol building. Lead deposits had been discovered in the mountain wilderness of southwestern Virginia, and Moses's contract stated he would be paid more if he built the roof with native Virginian lead. With help from his brother, he gained control over the lead mines and imported English miners and smelters, who knew how to extract the metal from the ore. In 1792, he and Mary moved to the mines and started a town, which he named for himself: Austinville. In this crude and remote place, Mary Austin gave birth on November 3, 1793, to their third child, a son, whom they named for Moses's brother and business partner, Stephen. The child's middle name was Fuller, the family name of some of Mary's relatives. A daughter, Emily, was born on June 22, 1795.

For his mining efforts, Moses Austin is credited with having founded the American lead industry, but he soon began losing large sums of money on his roofing

This 1836 portrait of Stephen F. Austin was created in
New Orleans by an artist whose name is not known today.
Austin is remembered for his many efforts on behalf of Texas
before, during, and immediately after Texas's revolution with
Mexico. He is considered the founder of Anglo-American Texas.

contract for the state capitol. In fact, he nearly went broke. Wanting to continue mining, Austin looked farther west for an opportunity. He had heard there were rich lead deposits in the Spanish province of Upper Louisiana, in the area we now know as Missouri. He visited these deposits on a long trip during the winter of 1796–1797. During this time, he left Mary at Austinville to manage both the family and the business, which she did very well.

Austin convinced the Spanish government to award him a contract to mine the lead, and he received a grant of 1 league of land, or 4,428 acres (1,792 ha) surrounding the area called Mine au Breton. In 1798, Moses moved his family to the Spanish village of Potosi. Stephen was then four and a half years old, and his sister, Emily, was almost three. Now a citizen of another

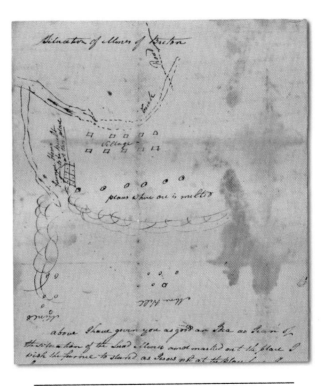

This drawing shows the layout of Moses Austin's frontier settlement at Mine au Breton, around 1798. Durham Hall appears at the bottom, and the mining project is in the center.

government, Moses Austin mined the rich ore and introduced modern smelting techniques. He soon made a fortune and controlled all the mines in the area. At one time he was worth nearly $200,000, a vast sum in those days. He built his family a southern-style mansion, that he called Durham Hall for his hometown in Connecticut.

Mary was known as Maria, although that might have been a nickname for her even before living in a Spanish province. In October 1803, she bore a second son, James Elijah Brown Austin, whom the family called Brown. Stephen was ten, and his father sent him east to a boarding school in Connecticut. Stephen was lonely and unhappy there, but Moses was determined to forge him into a man suitable to carry on his empire.

Also in 1803, the United States purchased Louisiana Territory from France, which had acquired it from Spain. The Austins were once again American citizens, and they were a family of power and influence. The American economy was in a slump, so to try to improve the frontier's troubled financial conditions, Moses Austin and others founded the Bank of St. Louis, which was the first bank west of the Mississippi River. The territorial governor and later president of the United States, William Henry Harrison, appointed Moses as a judge.

After three years in a Connecticut boarding school, and then some time spent visiting his family in Missouri, Stephen Austin was transferred to Transylvania University in Lexington, Kentucky, where he studied for two years. By the time he returned home to Potosi in 1810, he was a young man of seventeen. He was slender, with large brown eyes and curly brown hair that tended to go wild.

Years of being lectured to and badgered by his father in letters and during visits left Stephen well mannered, but shy and serious. Moses's demanding expectations were almost beyond belief. For example, when Stephen was only three, his father wrote him a thirty-page letter, for Stephen's "future use," detailing how Moses had succeeded in getting the Missouri grant. When Stephen was away at boarding school, he would wait for months to receive a letter from his father, and then when one came it

When Moses Austin came west, Mine au Breton lay in Spanish territory, but the mines themselves had been discovered by the French when the land was still part of Louisiana. The French still worked the mines, and they resented Moses's moving in and taking over. Moses built Durham Hall near the mining village in 1798. Native Americans resented the presence of white people on their land and attacked the village and the house in 1802. Moses defended his house with no help from the French. The town of Potosi was established at Mine au Breton in 1813, on land that Moses Austin had donated. Durham Hall was destroyed by fire in 1871.

This is a cameo of Stephen F. Austin at the age of twelve.
It was made soon after Austin reached Connecticut in 1804 to
attend school. The small portrait reveals a handsome boy with
good posture, wearing a stylish suit coat with wide lapels.

was full of lectures about how to behave and what kind of friends to keep. Moses even told Stephen that he was expected not just to succeed, but to become "a great man." Stephen adored his father and was desperate to please him, a fact that Moses Austin never seemed to appreciate.

When Stephen rejoined his family, however, he seemed to fulfill his father's hopes. He took over management of most of the family businesses, joined a local militia, and even served for six years in the territorial legislature. Then in 1819, a nationwide economic depression wiped out most of the family fortune. Moses Austin, nearly sixty years old, was ruined again and was faced with the necessity of starting again.

2. His Dying Father's Last Request

When he was twenty-seven years old, Stephen F. Austin went to Arkansas to find work. He seemed to land a good situation, qualifying as a district judge and being sworn in to office. At home in Missouri, his father continued to fret over how to restore the family fortune. Moses Austin had done well before by starting an American colony in Spanish Mexico. He began preparing to do so again, farther southwest in the province of Texas.

However, he now lacked even the means to get to Texas's provincial capital, San Antonio de Bexar, to set the scheme in motion. In October 1820, he visited Stephen in Little Rock, Arkansas. The dutiful son gave in and lent his father fifty dollars, a slave, a horse, and a mule to make the journey. Moses struck out west and entered San Antonio, which people also called Bexar, two days before Christmas.

Opposite: This 1816 map of what is now the United States of America was drawn by John Melish. The British and Spanish territories were contiguous, meaning they touched along their boundaries.

A colony is made up of a group of people who leave their mother country, travel to a distant country or a wilderness, and settle together. They keep their language, customs, and, usually, their loyalty to the old country. Over time, these ties may become faded, and the interests of the colonists may become different from those of the mother country. When the Pilgrims came to America from Britain in 1620, they started a colony. By 1776, their interests had become so different that they fought for and won their independence during the American Revolution. Stephen F. Austin and those who joined the Texas colony in the 1820s were Americans, but in their case, they agreed to become citizens of Mexico in exchange for receiving land on which to live. However, it took them only a few years to become unhappy with the Mexican political system, in which they had fewer rights than they had known at home. Because Texas was a nearly empty corner of Mexico, with a very small population, most Mexicans did not want to live there. Therefore, the officials who were sent were the worst the country had to offer. There were also big cultural differences that made the Americans long for their own government, in spite of the fact that Mexico had allowed them to settle in its territory.

The polite thing for Moses Austin to have done would have been to ask someone to let the governor know Austin desired a meeting. The brash Moses had little time for the formalities of Mexican society, however. He approached the governor, Antonio Martínez, directly and gave what today would be called a sales pitch. Martínez was horrified, first at Moses's boorish manners, and second because American adventurers had been sneaking into Texas and trying to set up shabby little empires for years. The governor ordered Moses Austin out of the country "with all possible speed." He wouldn't even read Austin's papers.

A stunned Moses left the governor's presence, unsure of what to do. Then, in an amazing stroke of luck, Moses ran into the Baron Felipe de Bastrop. They had met only briefly in New Orleans nearly twenty years before, yet they recognized each other and had a long visit. Unknown to Moses, Felipe de Bastrop was not really a baron. He was a Dutch tax collector named Bögel, who had fled from the Netherlands before he could be tried for stealing the taxes he had collected. In the following years, he had come to Texas and had reinvented himself as a Dutch nobleman. He was intelligent and had polished manners. He also had access to the most influential people in San Antonio. Austin explained his colony idea to Bastrop, who agreed to draw up a proper petition and present it to Governor Martínez. Bastrop would advise the governor to approve the plan.

This mural shows a gathering of Texas colonists in 1823
near the Colorado River, not far from the present town of
Bay City, Texas. Stephen F. Austin and Baron de
Bastrop (*seated*) are issuing land to the colonists.

Following the social rules proved to be a good idea. On the day after Christmas, Moses Austin was summoned. He learned that Governor Martínez had reversed his decision. He would send Moses's petition to a higher authority with the suggestion that Moses be allowed to start his colony.

Delighted, Moses started his journey home, but the several-hundred-mile (km) trip back began to go wrong almost at once. One of his traveling companions proved to be a black marketeer, one who traded in illegal goods. Moses, fearful of losing the government's favor, reported him to Bastrop. Then Moses's gunpowder got wet, so he couldn't hunt for food. It was midwinter, and the weather was freezing. For the final week of the journey, Moses and his slave had nothing to eat but roots and acorns. Moses Austin reached an inn near Natchitoches, Louisiana, on January 15, 1821, after suffering, he said, everything but death. Moses was sixty years old, which was an old age at that time. He was so sick and exhausted he couldn't leave his bed for three weeks. After resting, he traveled the rest of the way home to Missouri.

While his father was in Mexico, Stephen left the Arkansas Territory and moved to New Orleans, Louisiana, even though he had just been appointed a judge. Perhaps he found that the work did not suit him, or maybe he was trying to move farther away from his father's influence. He also owed money to people in Missouri, so perhaps he moved in an attempt to get some distance from them. Certainly he hoped to find work to support himself, but instead he discovered that business in New Orleans was as bad as it was everywhere else. "I offered to hire myself out as a clerk," he wrote his mother, "as an overseer, or anything else, but business here is too dull." In fact he discovered that some young men there were taking jobs just to be paid in room and board, without even asking for money.

In Missouri, Stephen's father should have realized that his chances of starting an American colony in Texas were not good. Governor Martínez did not have the last word on whether Moses could proceed. Final permission would have to come from Texas's military commander, Joaquín de Arredondo, a soldier who was always fearful of revolutions and who had crushed two of them in earlier years. Instead of waiting for word from Arredondo and resting to get well, Moses Austin busied himself signing up settlers to return with him to Texas. He was ready to go to Texas even without approval.

His optimism turned out to be justified. In May 1821, Moses Austin received wonderful news. Arredondo had approved the colony, because Spain's new king had approved a constitution that allowed former subjects to resettle. Under the terms of the contract, Moses would receive nearly $20,000 in fees from his colonists, in addition to his own large grant of land. He was beside himself with joy. On May 22, he wrote to

This is a transcript of a letter written by Stephen F. Austin to his mother, Maria, on January 20, 1821. Maria gave Stephen much love and attention as he grew up. Perhaps, historians think, she was trying to make up for the demands placed on Stephen by his strict father.

Stephen, "I can now go forward with confidence, and I hope and pray that you will discharge your doubts as to the enterprise. Raise your spirits. Times are changing, and a new chance presents itself."

Stephen read this letter in New Orleans and realized that his father meant for him to come and take part in the colony. This was not good news, for Stephen had finally found a good job, helping to edit a newspaper. Even better, he had met a lawyer named Joseph Hawkins, whose brother Stephen had known at Transylvania University. They became friends, and Hawkins offered to pay Stephen's expenses while he studied law and learned French, which was commonly spoken in New Orleans. Stephen was impressed and grateful. He wrote home that "an offer so generous, and from a man who two months ago was a stranger to me, has almost made me change my opinion of the human race."

Instead of giving Stephen the freedom to make his own decisions, Moses instead wrote him that, if Hawkins had that kind of money, Stephen should talk him into investing in the colony. Stephen received further word from his father, instructing him to send a shipload of supplies to the mouth of the Colorado River in Texas for a new capital city, which Moses was going to call Austina. Moses Austin, however, was working himself to death. He had never recovered his strength after his journey, and he had refused to rest in the months since the terrible ordeal of that trip. Stephen suddenly received news from home that Moses was dangerously ill with pneumonia.

The Spanish government had sent a delegation to meet Moses Austin at Natchitoches, the place from where most Americans left when they went into Mexico. Stephen had to go meet them instead. Soon after he boarded a riverboat to go there, word came from Hawkins that Moses Austin had died, and he forwarded a letter from Stephen's mother.

Shortly before the end, Maria Austin wrote to Stephen, "He drew me down to him and with much distress and difficulty of speech, told me it was too late, that he was going . . . he begged me to tell you to take his place dear Stephen that it is his dying father's last request to prosecute the enterprise he had commenced." Stephen agreed to carry on.

Moses Austin had not been exaggerating Mexico's willingness to settle Americans in Texas. Governor Martínez sent a high-level delegation to Natchitoches to meet Austin. The delegation included the *alcalde*, or mayor, of San Antonio, Juan Erasmo Seguín, and San Antonio native Juan Martín de Veramendi, who later became governor.

For many years people believed that Stephen F. Austin was not enthusiastic about taking over his father's Texas venture, and that he did so only to honor Moses's last wish. However, a recently discovered letter that he wrote

Juan Erasmo Seguín (1782–1857) was a political figure and businessman in San Antonio. In 1821, Governor Antonio Martínez appointed him to inform Moses Austin that the latter's petition to start a colony in Texas was approved. Seguín developed business and personal ties to Stephen F. Austin, who often stayed with the Seguín family during his travels.

to a friend indicates that he was, in fact, looking forward to the venture and was in high spirits. Historians might have been mistaken all these years in believing Austin did not want to carry on his father's work. Perhaps Austin really was reluctant to work at colonization but tried to appear enthusiastic because he didn't want to be stuck in Texas alone and hoped to influence others to join him.

Austin, Seguín, and Veramendi left for San Antonio in early July, along with a party of men Austin brought to help him explore places in Texas where they might start the colony. When Governor Martínez met Austin, the governor was impressed, calling him a young man

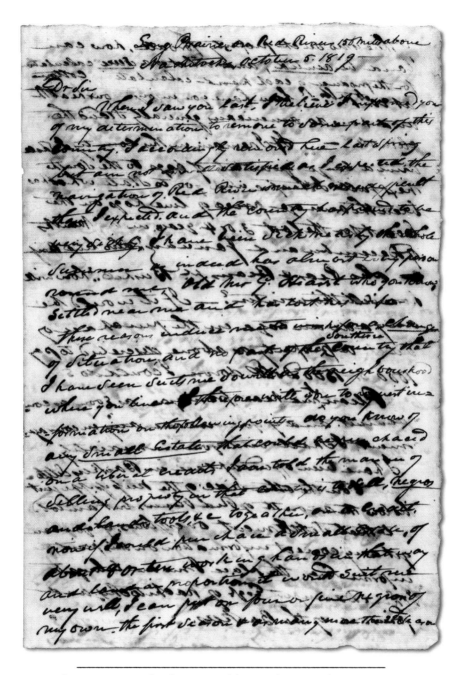

This is a recently discovered letter that Stephen F. Austin wrote about his 1821 trip to Texas to a friend named Jacob Pettit. Austin and Pettit knew each other from having served together in the Missouri militia.

Stephen F. Austin owned these pistols
and this tomahawk. The tomahawk, a small ax,
first belonged to Moses Austin, who carried
it on his initial trip to Texas in 1820.

"of high honor, of scrupulous regard for formality, and of desiring to learn how to discharge faithfully the duties proposed by his late father." The younger Austin also gained the friendship of his father's connection in Spanish Mexico, the self-appointed Baron de Bastrop, who proved himself very valuable.

Austin was in San Antonio for nine days, working out the details of the settlement plan. Each man who came into his Texan colony would receive 640 acres (259 ha) of land, and additional land would be issued if he had a wife and children. Martínez permitted Austin to explore the valley of the Colorado River all the way to the coast to find land on which to locate his colony. At that time, there was only one other town built in Texas, named La Bahía. This town was located about 80 miles (129 km) southwest of San Antonio. There Austin obtained a guide, but still they got lost. Austin explored the Guadalupe River before reaching the Colorado River. After exploring the Colorado River, he moved eastward to explore the Brazos River.

He found unpopulated land, rich and fertile almost beyond belief. Game was abundant, and vegetation was thick and lush. If he had had any doubts about carrying on his father's work before, he now was seized with the

In this engraving by J. T. Hammond, four colonists thread their way through a field of sugar cane in Texas. Because the soil was considerably fertile in this area, vegetation often grew very high. This engraving appeared in the 1834 publication *A Visit to Texas*.

grand idea of bringing American civilization into this vacant wilderness and letting it take root. It was a vision that quickly consumed him. He was doing it to show that enlightened and honest men could remake a wilderness. He said his only ambition was for a "modest independence." He was not doing it to make money. "I can with truth and a clear conscience say that," he wrote. Rather, he "commenced on the solid basis of . . . integrity."

Back in Natchitoches in late fall, he found about one hundred letters waiting for him from Americans who wanted to join his colony in Texas. It was clear that the colony would be successful, and that many people were ready to go, but he had many things to do to arrange his affairs in New Orleans before he could join them. Austin turned to a friend from his Missouri days, Josiah Bell, to lead the first American settlers into Mexico and to prepare a place until he could join them. After years of drifting and discontentment, Stephen F. Austin was certain he had found his life's passion.

3. The Texas Dream

Stephen F. Austin's dream, to settle the vast territory of Texas, was perhaps one of the loftiest dreams in North America. Austin became so consumed with his Texas venture that he quickly went against his own instincts and did what his father once had advised him to do. He asked his friend Hawkins to invest in the colony. Austin sold Hawkins half of his interest in the whole business for $4,000. Hawkins would become Austin's agent, handling correspondence and publicity for the Texas venture. With Hawkins's $4,000 Austin purchased supplies and loaded them onto a small ship called the *Lively*. He sent the ship to the mouth of the Colorado River, where Josiah Bell and the other colonists were waiting. The crew of the *Lively* mistook the Brazos River for the Colorado River, waited awhile but were met by no one, so they returned to New Orleans. When the *Lively* went back out for a second try, it was wrecked on Galveston Island and all of its cargo was lost. Even worse, while the *Lively* was trying to find its way, Austin returned to San Antonio to make final plans with Governor Martínez and received shocking

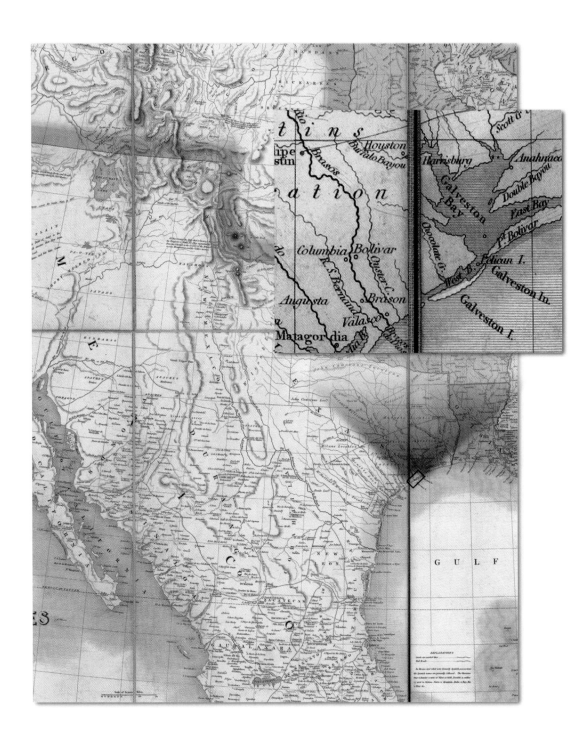

news. There had been a revolution in Mexico. Native Mexicans had been trying for ten years to throw out the royal Spanish government, and they had finally succeeded. The Spanish were no longer in control. A man named Agustín de Iturbide was in charge, and Austin's contract had been thrown out. This change threatened all of Austin's plans. There was no alternative, so Austin had to travel more than 1,000 miles (1,609 km) to Mexico City, to try to fix the situation.

Austin let Bell know what was going on and then set off with a few traveling companions. They arrived in Mexico City in April 1822, and found the city, as he wrote, "in an unsettled state, the whole people and country still agitated by the revolution. . . . Party spirit raging." His own situation could hardly have been worse. He and his companions were, he wrote, "without acquaintances, without friends, ignorant of the language, of the laws, the forms, the disposition and feelings of the Government, with barely the means of paying my expenses."

With his usual determination, Austin set to work teaching himself Spanish while patiently waiting for officials to see him so he could convince them to support his contract. More important, he realized the advantage of learning and accepting the customs of another

Opposite: This 1839 map, drawn by David H. Burr, shows the United States of America and parts of neighboring countries. The map features state boundaries, as well as cities, roads, trails, canals, and railroads. The pullout in the top right corner shows Galveston Island. This island is boxed in red on the main map.

culture, something that was beyond the ability of most Americans of his day. It was fortunate that he behaved so well and made many friends, because politics in Mexico City soon spun wildly out of control. Iturbide was made emperor, and the Mexican congress would not go against him to help Austin. As soon as Austin was able to change the emperor's mind and had obtained a new colonial agreement, the emperor was overthrown and later shot. The new congress again threw out the contract. At this point, most men would have given up and gone home. With patience and persistence, Austin succeeded beyond his wildest dreams. His long months in Mexico City had won him great respect, and in April 1823, he reached a final agreement with the new government. Austin was to settle three hundred families in his colony, each of whom would receive 1 *league* of land, or 4,428 acres (1,792 ha), for ranching, and a *labor* of land, 177 acres (72 ha), for farming. Moreover, because the central government could not oversee the colony, Austin was allowed to charge each of his colonists 12 ½ cents per acre (5 cents/ha) to survey their grants and to provide for the defense of the colony. In addition, he was granted some 100,000 acres (40,469 ha) of his own land. The government would not collect taxes from the colony for six years. Each new Texan was required to become a Roman Catholic, but religious practice would not be strictly enforced. Austin would be *empresario*, a general

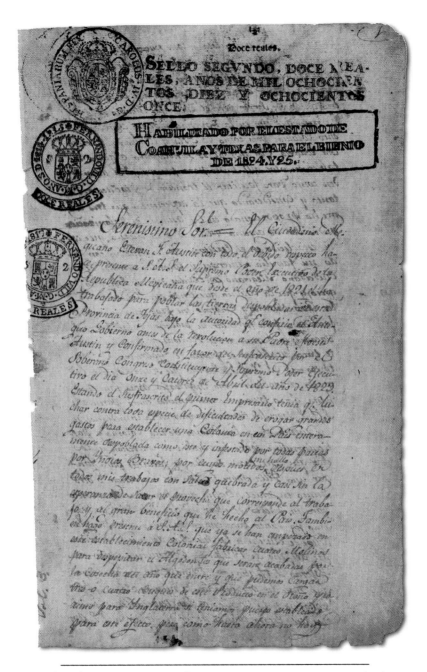

This document states the important agreement reached in April 1823 between Stephen F. Austin and the Mexican congress. Stephen would be permitted to settle three hundred families in his colony in Texas and to lead them.

manager of broad powers and with limited oversight from the government. It was a stunning victory for him.

When Austin returned to Bell and the others on the Brazos River in August 1823, he had been gone for one and a half years. Some of the colonists had lost hope and had gone home, but Austin had no difficulty filling his obligation to bring three hundred families into Texas. He established a capital city for his colony, San Felipe de Austin, on the Brazos well up from the river's mouth. He issued a set of laws and simple court rules, although there was little crime at this time. This was because Austin required all his colonists to produce sworn statements of their good character before he let them in the colony. Finally he set about starting an economy based on growing cotton.

Austin was very practical in the way he governed his colony. He outlawed gambling, for instance, but he allowed horse racing. He knew that people who wanted to win races would find ways to breed faster and healthier horses for working their farms. Most of his daily work was issuing land titles, which he did with Bastrop.

Word soon spread in the United States of the ideal world Austin was creating. Several members of his own family, including his sister, Emily, and her husband,

---

Opposite: This 1823 proclamation was given by Stephen F. Austin to the families settling in Texas. It outlined the laws by which he expected the settlers to live. The document, which bears Stephen's handwritten corrections, also urged the settlers to uphold their Christian values.

To the settlers in Austins settlement.

FELLOW CITIZENS,

After an absence of sixteen months I have the pleasure of returning once more to the settlement which it has been the labor of the last three years of my life to establish in the unsettled deserts of this province. Nothing but the interest of the settlers, and the general welfare of the settlement could have induced me to make the sacrifices of time, of fatigue and money, which this enterprize has cost me; but feeling in honor bound never to abandon those who had embarked with me, and animated with the hope of rendering an important service to the great Mexican nation, and particularly to this Province, by the formation of a flourishing colony within its limits, I have persevered through all the difficulties created by the political convulsions of the last year, and now have the satisfaction of announcing that every necessary power relative to the formation of the colony is granted to me by the Supreme Executive power and Sovereign Congress of Mexico; and that I shall immediately commence in conjunction with the Baron de Bastrop, the governmental Commissioner appointed for this purpose, to designate the land for the settlers, and deliver complete titles therefor.

It will be observed, by all who wish to be received into this colony, that the conditions indicated by me in the first commencement of the settlement must be complied with, and particularly that the most unquestionable testimony of good character, and industrous and moral habits will be required. No person can be permitted to remain in the settlement longer than may be absolutely necessary to prepare for a removal who does not exhibit such testimony. This regulation is in conformity with the orders of the Superior Government, and will be enforced with the utmost rigour.

Being charged by the Superior Government with the administration of justice, the punishment of crimes, and the preservation of good order and tranquility within the settlement, it will be my study to devote that attention to those subjects which their transcendant importance requires, and I confidently hope that, with the aid of the settlers we shall be able to present an example of industry and good morals equally creditable to ourselves and gratifying to the government of our adoption.

The Alcaldes appointed on the Colorado and Brazos in the month of November last will continue to exercise their functions until the year for which they were elected expires, at which time a new election for those officers will be ordered. The administration of justice by the Alcaldes will be subject to my inspection; and appeals from their decisions will be decided by me. Fixed regulations will be established on this subject, and made known to the

the correctness of his own conduct. Honest and industrious men may live together all their lives without a law-suit or difference with each other. I have known examples of this kind in the United States: so it must be with us—nothing is more easy: all that is necessary is for every one to attend industriously to his own business, and in all cases follow the great and sacred christian rule, *to do unto others as you wish them to do unto you.* As regards the suppression of vice and immorality, and the punishment of crime, much depends on yourselves. The wisest laws and the most efficient administration of justice, in criminal cases, avails but little, unless seconded by the good examples, patriotism and virtues of the people. It will therefore be expected that every man in the settlement will at all times be willing to aid the civil authority whenever called on to pursue, apprehend or punish criminals, and also, that the most prompt information will be given to the nearest civil officer, of any murder, robbery, breach of the peace, or other violation of the laws.

Being also charged with the Commission of Lt. Coronel Commandant of the Militia within the settlement, I shall, as soon as possible, organize a battalion of militia, in which every man capable of bearing arms must be enrolled and hold himself in readiness to march at a moment's warning, whenever called on to repel the attacks of hostile indians or other enemies of the Mexican nation.

I am limited to the number of 300 families for the settlement on the Colorado and Brazos. The government have ordered that all over that number who are introduced by me, must settle in the interior of the province, near the ancient establishments.

As soon as the necessary information can be procured, a town will be established as the capital of the settlement, and a port of entry will be designated on the coast for the introduction of all articles required for the use of the settlers All town scites are reserved, and no person will be permitted to locate them.

Fellow Citizens, let me again repeat that your happiness rests with yourselves; the Mexican Government have been bountiful in the favors and privileges which she has granted to the settlement, in return for which all she asks is that you will be firm supporters and defenders of the Independence and Liberty of the Mexican Nation; that you should industriously cultivate the soil that is granted you, that you should strictly obey the laws and constituted authorities, and in fact, that you should be good citizens and virtuous men.

STEPHEN F. AUSTIN

Province of Texos, July, 1823.

The remaining portion of the Peach Point compound, shown above, consists of just two rooms. The building is displayed to visitors on special occasions by its present owners. This photo was taken on June 28, 1940.

Stephen F. Austin's sister, Emily Austin Perry, and her husband, James Perry, took up residence in Texas on August 31, 1831. Austin designed a large house as a family compound on the Peach Point Plantation. He named the plantation for the wild peach trees growing there. Although the Austin residence appeared to be a single-family dwelling, it actually concealed separate apartments for different family members. The house was almost totally destroyed by a hurricane in 1909. The two rooms that survived on the east side of the house were the same two that Stephen Austin lived in when in residence at Peach Point. They continue to be furnished with Austin family heirlooms.

James Perry, came to Texas and settled in a kind of family compound at Peach Point, along the Brazos River near the Texas Gulf coast. Austin's mother, Maria, was to join them, but she died in Missouri before making the journey. Austin was greatly attached to his older cousin, Mary Austin Holley, who lived in Lexington, Kentucky. He was overjoyed when she came to Texas for a visit.

Austin's contract held him personally responsible for the conduct of his settlers. For a time, Austin was able to ensure that his colony was settled by people who were moral and hardworking. Many of them were extremely well educated. In fact, one traveler was shocked to hear a farmer reciting Latin lessons while feeding his hogs!

Texas's famous cattle industry lay many years in the future. There were thousands of wild longhorn cattle everywhere. They were descended from cows that had escaped from early Spanish explorers, but few people bothered to herd them. Game was abundant, and most meat was obtained by hunting. Austin's cousin Mary was amazed by the generosity of the colonists in sharing what they had hunted. "There is a peculiar feeling among them about game," she wrote. "No one will receive money for any thing taken with his gun, but will cheerfully give you as much as you will take, and feel insulted, if you offer him money in return."

Life was not always easy, though. In a way, the women had it the worst. The men got to explore and to

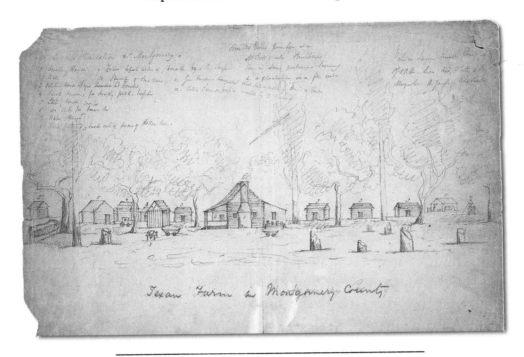

William Bollaert, a British traveler, drew this early Texan farmstead in Montgomery City while visiting Texas. The buildings stand among the stumps of the trees that were used to construct them. Writing above the drawing identifies most of the smaller cabins as slave quarters.

hunt. It was the women who mostly missed friends and family back home. The women were stuck keeping house, and they had few resources with which to do their work. Texas, wrote one wit, was heaven for men and dogs, but hell for women and oxen.

When Austin's cousin Mary returned to Kentucky, she wrote a book of practical advice for those considering a move to Texas. Fancy clothing, she said, was not needed, but people should bring all the plain clothing they could, for replacements were hard to get. She also said, "Those who *must* have a feather-bed had better bring it themselves, for . . . though the air swarms with live geese, a feather-bed could not be got for love or money."

The principal food crop was corn. People were just beginning to plant cotton to sell for cash. Wheat was almost unheard of, and most wheat flour had to be shipped in from the United States. When it could be found at all, it cost a precious ten dollars per barrel. In fact, some children grew up eating only bread that was made from cornmeal. There was one boy who didn't know what biscuits made from wheat flour were, the first time he saw them. He poked a little stick through their centers and made the biscuits into wheels for a toy cart.

Mary Austin Holley developed a close relationship with her cousin Stephen when she came to Texas in 1827. Stephen approved of her idea to write a book about Texas, because it would give accurate information in print to those thinking of settling in the new colony.

The health of people in the area was not always good. Mosquitoes were thick in summer, and malaria was common. Sometimes another disease, called yellow fever, caused terrible suffering and killed many people. There were few doctors, and the ones available could do little to help people due to lack of supplies.

When Austin issued land grants to his colonists, he was careful that each piece of land had frontage on a river so the settlers could buy supplies and could sell their crops to passing riverboats. There were few roads in Texas, and they could not be used in bad weather. There was almost no money, so cotton, cowhides, or corn were taken in exchange. Merchants in the United States would advertise in Texas what they had to sell and what dates they expected to be at different land-ings. A merchant named G. H. Harrison placed the following advertisement in a Texas newspaper:

"TO THE PLANTERS ON THE BRAZOS:
I will have up by the Steam Boat Lady Byron, from 150 to 200 barrels of freight, consisting of every article that the farmers want; such as cof-fee, sugar, molasses, flour, salt, tobacco, bagging and rope, shoes, boots, hats, domestics, woolens, nails, soap, rice, teas, powder and lead, &c., &c. All of which I will sell for a very small advance on Galveston prices, for cash, cotton or hides. Persons wishing to purchase will do well to have their cotton on the bank of the river, as I am determined to sell during the trip."

In 1824, the Baron de Bastrop left the colony to take a seat in the state legislature. Even though he was not really a baron and so was living a lie, he had served the colony well. Austin needed a new secretary and right-hand man. He chose Samuel May Williams, the son of a Rhode Island sea captain. Williams was twenty-eight, two years younger than Austin, and had perfect manners and beautiful handwriting, a great asset in a time when all office work was done by hand. In a short time, the two became best friends. Williams issued land titles and ran the colony when Austin was away. Austin's power as empresario gave him the right to award extra

This page from Stephen F. Austin's ledger, or account book, reveals that a man named Clement Dyer was granted 4,428 acres (1,792 ha) for ranching and 265 acres (107 ha) for farming. The thin ledger paper allowed writing on the reverse side to show through.

This painting of Samuel May Williams dates from about 1836.
Williams, who worked closely with Austin, was a businessman,
a land speculator, and a banker. He was regarded
as the father of the Texas navy.

land to citizens who brought money and various skills to the colony, and Austin gave Williams nearly 50,000 acres (20,234 ha), which Williams selected from some of the richest and most valuable land.

The state legislature, which met in Saltillo, Mexico, had begun allowing other empresarios to start American settlements in Texas, and Austin's colony was now one of several. In fact, he and Williams, as partners, applied for and received the right to start more colonies. By 1830, Texas was home to thousands and thousands of Americans. Although Austin was the empresario of only four of these colonies, all Americans in Texas knew that it was Austin whose work had allowed them to be there.

4. The Texas Nightmare

For a while, life in Stephen F. Austin's Texas was peaceful and prosperous. In time, however, word began to spread in the United States, especially in the South, of the vast tracts, or pieces, of land that were available for only a little trouble. People began sneaking into Texas and squatting, or settling on vacant land that they believed no one would claim. Austin was able to run a number of squatters off, but soon the trickle became a flood. People in trouble with the law in the United States came to Texas to hide, which polluted the area with dangerous and immoral people. Also, the Mexican government granted colonies to other empresarios besides Austin, and some of them were less particular about who they let stay on their lands. In fact, throughout the South it was said that the initials G. T. T. scratched on the door of an empty cabin meant "Gone To Texas." Often people left just in time to

Opposite: This 1837 map of Texas, based on one drawn by Stephen F. Austin, outlines the land grants given to settlers. The list at bottom left mentions 14,050 families, of which 11,300 were on Austin's land.

MAP
OF
TEXAS
With Parts of the Adjoining States

COMPILED BY STEPHEN F. AUSTIN

PUBLISHED BY H. S. TANNER Philadelphia

avoid arrest. The situation became more and more diffi-cult for Austin to control as the newcomers began com-mitting crimes in Texas.

Many Americans who came into Texas that way had little patience or sympathy with the Mexican political and legal systems. If Texas was settled by Americans, they believed, then it ought to belong to Americans, and they began arguing that Texas should split from Mexico and be free to annex, or join, herself to the United States. Austin knew how dangerous such talk was, and he some-times referred to the American squatters in contempt as "leatherstockings," after a backwoods character in popu-lar novels of the day.

Austin's power over his people was almost absolute during his colony's first six years. Austin was not com-fortable exercising such power. Late in 1827, a new state constitution went into effect, and Austin saw to it that the settlements each elected an *ayuntamiento*, or town coun-cil, to take over governmental authority. Austin knew that even without power he would still hold great influ-ence in representing his people to the Mexican govern-ment. Once his word was no longer law, however, the sit-uation with squatters became even worse.

Real trouble actually had begun the year before, when an empresario in east Texas named Haden Edwards got into an election dispute with the government. On December 21, 1826, Edwards declared his colony inde-pendent of Mexico. The Mexican government was against

This undated photo shows Texas empresario Haden Edwards. He was educated for the law but was more interested in land speculation.

such a move. A little more than a month later, Mexican troops, as well as Austin and militia from his colony, reached Edwards's capital of Nacogdoches, and the little revolution collapsed. Austin involved his colony to demonstrate his loyalty to the Mexican government.

The growing hostility of Texan residents alarmed the Mexican government. It decided to send one of its best army officers, General Manuel de Mier y Terán, on an inspection through Texas to report on the conditions there. The general quickly saw Anglo-Hispanic tensions building and knew that if things continued in this way, Mexico could not prevent Texas from separating and joining the United States. Mier y Terán recommended strongly that Mexico find a way to get more Mexican settlers into Texas, and also that Mexico forbid any further emigration from the United States. By keeping the population mostly Mexican, their sheer numbers would work in Mexico's favor in the event of war. His suggestions were adopted in a fateful law, the *Ley* of April 6, 1830, which forbade further colonists from entering Texas from the United States. Adoption of the ley left Americans in

Texas feeling frightened, angry, and cut off from ties to the United States.

Austin saw disaster looming and quickly used his good influence with the government to have his and a neighboring colony exempted from the ley. He also knew he had to begin working to get the law repealed, but before he could do that the situation worsened.

The Texas colonies' exemption from Mexican taxes, which was part of the original colonization deal, was set to expire. The government sent two men to collect seaport duties. The men were American adventurers who had Hispanicized their names and had gone into Mexican service: John (Juan) Davis Bradburn and his tax collector George (Jorge) Fisher. They were arrogant and probably corrupt, and they enraged the people around the port town of Anáhuac, where they were sent to collect taxes. Stephen F. Austin met several times with Bradburn to get him to lighten up, but was unable to influence him. Austin saw the situation spinning out of control. "I had an ignorant, whimsical, selfish and suspicious set of rulers over me," he later wrote, "a perplexed, confused colonization law to execute, and an unruly set of frontier North American republicans to control who felt . . . that they were beyond the arm of government or of law."

In May 1832, Bradburn began arresting people he suspected of being troublemakers, and about 150 outraged colonists took up arms and captured his troops. The colonists' clashing against Bradburn's troops, known as

one of the Anáhuac Disturbances, was treason. The colonists could be shot for treason but saw a way to avoid being charged. From Anáhuac, the Texans retreated a short distance to Turtle Bayou, a Texas waterway, to consider what to do. Mexico was in another civil war, and the government that sent Bradburn appeared to be losing to a popular general named Antonio López de Santa Anna. The Texans passed resolutions while camped on Turtle Bayou, announcing their support for Santa Anna, and as he came closer to winning the civil war, danger to the Texans passed. Stephen F. Austin cautiously supported these moves, but it thrust him right into the middle of Mexican politics, which he had always avoided.

Through all this, Austin remained loyal to Mexico, which caused many independence-minded Texans to resent him. They began holding a series of political conventions to decide what to do. Austin participated in these conventions, but his aim was to control their action, not to support their moves toward independence. Santa Anna, whom the Texans had supported, became president of Mexico in March 1833, the very time that a convention in Texas asked for separate Mexican statehood for Texas. Texas had long been joined as a province to Coahuila, but the Constitution of 1824 had promised

Previous page: This 1839 map, drawn by David H. Burr, shows the United States of America and parts of neighboring countries. The map features state boundaries, as well as cities, towns, roads, trails, canals, and railroads. Anáhuac is outlined in blue.

Antonio López de Santa Anna became president of Mexico
in 1833 through a democratic election. However, he quickly
pronounced himself dictator. He is known as the leading villain
of Texas history. This undated portrait of Santa Anna was
painted by an artist whose name is not known today.

This portrait of Stephen F. Austin and his dog was painted by the British artist William Howard in Mexico City in 1833, shortly before Austin's arrest on suspicion of trying to incite a revolt in Texas. The portrait is painted on ivory in watercolors.

Texas eventual statehood of its own. The delegates even drafted a state constitution. Austin was sent off to Mexico City to present the petitions to Santa Anna. Austin held no political office, but he was still the most influential man in the province and enjoyed wide respect in the Mexican capital.

Once Austin met with Santa Anna, it was clear to Austin that the president was not what he had claimed to be. Santa Anna had sought power as a liberal and as a federalist, or one who believes that power should be given to the states from a central authority. In truth, he aimed to become a centralist dictator. Austin quickly perceived Santa Anna's real intentions.

In anger and frustration, Austin wrote a letter to friends on the ayuntamiento of San Antonio, advising them to go ahead and organize Texas as a state without waiting for the government to act. It was an incredible mistake. Most of the Hispanics on the town council at San Antonio were loyal to Santa Anna, and when they received Austin's letter, they sent it straight to the government. The letter would not reach Santa Anna immediately, though.

In further talks with Santa Anna, Austin finally won a few concessions, enough to allow him to return home having accomplished something. On his journey home to Texas, Austin had gone as far as Saltillo when suddenly he was arrested and hauled in chains back to Mexico City. Austin was charged with sedition, or writing something that encouraged people to be disloyal to the government. Actually he had committed no crime, and no court would even hear his case, but Santa Anna had him moved from jail to jail. From this unfair treatment, Austin saw that he had been correct in his hunch that Santa Anna was just a dictator. Austin was held in some form of detention, either in prison or under house arrest, until July 1835. By the time he returned to Texas, he had been gone for two years and four months, and he was a changed man—sick, bitter, angry, and ready to join his fellow Texans in a war for independence.

5. Revolution

While Austin was imprisoned in Mexico, affairs back in Texas grew ever worse. A powerful political faction, or group, that wanted a war for independence gained influence. This group was headed by the brothers William and John Wharton, who had caused problems for Austin by calling for a separation from Mexico ever since they had arrived in Texas. The Whartons called for a consultation of the people to meet and to decide on independence, but with Austin's sudden return, people wanted to hear his views on the subject. However, Austin's unex-

This is a portrait of William Harris Wharton (1802–1839). Wharton's argument for Texas's complete independence from Mexico went against Austin's milder views.

pected agreement that war was now their only choice made the meeting happen quickly. The argument was not about whether to fight, but what to fight for. The Whartons were for independence, but Austin wanted to fight to restore the Mexican constitution of 1824, which Santa Anna had cancelled after making himself dictator.

This argument was forgotten during the outbreak of the Texas Revolution on October 2, 1835. One hundred Mexican dragoons, or heavily armed infantry, were sent to disarm the town of Gonzales of its cannons, which were used for defense against hostile Native American groups. The townspeople angrily refused to give up the cannons and made a banner that read, "Come And Take It." Volunteers streamed in from all the colonies and defeated the dragoons in a quick battle.

This is a re-creation of the Come and Take It banner that was flown during the outbreak of the Texas Revolution. The original banner has been lost.

After the fight at Gonzales, other Texan volunteer groups defeated Mexican units and forced them to retreat into San Antonio. In mid-October, the Texans had San Antonio under siege, and Austin joined his men there. The volunteers made Austin the general of their army, even though he had never been a soldier. Once he was with them, the soldiers wouldn't let him out of their sight, as they feared he might try again to make peace with the Mexicans. Austin was their general, but in a way he was also their prisoner. Austin had been made general simply because he was the only person in the colonies capable of unifying others, and because he was the Texans' best hope for obtaining international help.

On November 1, he wrote a letter to the Mexican general in San Antonio, Martín Perfecto de Cos, telling him to surrender. The Mexican commander returned it, unread, along with an insulting note that he would not correspond with rebels. Austin then explored San Antonio's defensive positions and was surprised to discover them "much stronger than has been supposed." It also worried him that his army was composed of volunteers who did not obey orders unless they wanted to. They were also running out of supplies.

The city of San Antonio was too well defended to take by storm, so Austin's officers advised him to keep up the siege until their own force could grow stronger. Austin also sent out cavalry patrols to make sure his army was not surprised by any more Mexican troops. Austin's

This portrait of Mexican general Martín Perfecto de Cos, possibly styled after a painting done by William H. Croome around 1848, appears in John Frost's 1869 *Pictorial History of Mexico and the Mexican War*. General Cos helped to provoke the Texas Revolution by demanding the surrender of Texan cannons. This resulted in the Battle of Gonzales.

volunteers, however, had come for a fight, not to play a waiting game. Within a short time, about two hundred of them deserted him and returned home, leaving him with a meager force of about six hundred. Many of those who remained were constantly drunk. Austin was horrified. He posted a guard to patrol the camp at night, as much to keep the men from leaving as to watch for a Mexican attack, and he begged Texas's temporary government to make sure that no more whiskey found its way to the army. "If there is any on the road," he wrote, "turn it back."

The government to which Austin wrote, however, was in almost as much chaos as the army. When the government, called the Consultation, first met, so few men showed up that they could not even conduct business. Most of the delegates were with Austin and the army, and another of the delegates, Sam Houston, rode out from the capital to fetch them. Houston was already a frontier legend, a former governor of Tennessee who had fought under Andrew Jackson many years before. He was famous as a soldier and as a politician, but he was even more famous as an unstable drunk whose wife had left him, and he occasionally lived with Native Americans.

Although the six hundred soldiers who remained with Austin were suspicious of him because he had remained loyal to Mexico longer than they had, they were even more suspicious of Houston. Houston told them they were undisciplined. He wanted them to retreat over

This is a photograph of the Sam Houston Memorial in Houston, Texas. Sam Houston is one of the most written about heroes in American history. He is remembered for being especially good at leading men and at winning political elections.

When Sam Houston entered Texas on December 2, 1832, he was already one of the best-known men in the United States. He was born in Virginia in 1793, and was raised in Tennessee. He joined the U.S. Army at age twenty and distinguished himself in battle against the Creek Native Americans. His commander, General Andrew Jackson, was impressed and began guiding Houston's career. Houston served two terms as a congressman before being elected governor of Tennessee. Once Jackson became president, many thought Houston might succeed him. However, there was a scandal when Houston's wife left him. Socially and politically ruined, Houston went west in 1829 to the Indian Territory and lived with Native Americans for three years. During this time, he became an alcoholic, was held up to national ridicule, and made powerful political enemies. In 1832, he pulled himself together, and Jackson sent him to Texas to begin scheming about how to separate it from Mexico. Houston served two terms as president of the Republic of Texas, and after Texas became a state, he served thirteen years in Washington, D.C., as a senator. In 1859, he was elected governor of Texas but was removed from office in 1861 when he supported the Union rather than the Confederacy.

ground they had already won, then reorganize and drill to become a real army. They clamored to have Austin address them and give his opinion. Austin's nephew wrote that the general was so sick he could barely climb onto his horse to speak to the men, but from his saddle he agreed with his men that they should stay and fight where they were. He did agree with Houston, however, that the army needed discipline more than anything else, but he could not say it in front of the men. Had he done so, many more of them would have deserted.

At Austin's urging, those volunteers who had been elected to the Consultation reluctantly followed Sam Houston back to San Felipe. Austin and Houston had disagreed on whether the army should fall back to reorganize, but they were of one mind about the need for the government to get its act together. "The country must have organization," Austin wrote in a letter he sent after Houston. "Promptness and energy in the Consultation is all important. All depends on it."

One faction in the government wanted immediate independence from Mexico; the other wanted to continue pressing for Mexican statehood. After fierce debate, the government appointed Sam Houston commander of all the Texan forces. They believed that Austin would be most useful if they sent him to the United States to raise money and to get supplies. On November 18, Austin learned that he was being relieved of command. He kept the information a secret,

Before Bexar Nov. 22 1835.

Dr Brother,
My health has been very bad since I left the cibolo, more than a month ago, and I have been unable to attend personally to the duties of my station with that activity which the service required — I believe however that all has been done, that could have been — I have at various times submitted the question of storming the fortifications to a council of officers, and they have uniformly decided against it — Yesterday I was in hopes, the army was prepared to do it, and I issued a positive order, to storm at day light this morning, but on trial I found it impossible to get half the men willing for the measure, and it was abandoned from necessity

I begin to doubt whether much more can be done here, than to leave a force in winter quarters at the missions below town, say 250 men, untill the necessary regular force & guns & other supplies come out—

My health is better than it has been and is improving fast — I shall make another effort to get the army to storm, if it cannot be effected, I shall leave as many as will stay in winter quarters and go to the U. S.—

This is a letter written by Austin to his sister Emily's husband, James Franklin Perry. In his letter, Austin describes the difficulties he has had as army supervisor, and he complains about his army's lack of organization.

believing that the army would collapse if they learned he was leaving.

The Texan forces finally received some cannons, and to try to unify the army, Austin ordered an assault on San Antonio for the morning of November 23. To his shock, only a few men agreed to obey the order, and he had to cancel it. "I have done the best I could," he wrote to his sister Emily's husband, but "this army . . . is without proper organization—The volunteer system will not do for such a service, I have had a hard and difficult task to perform, and am really so worn out." He had never even pretended to be a military man, he continued, and he believed that the government had acted wisely in naming him a commissioner to go to the United States to try to get help.

On November 24, Austin reviewed his troops for the last time. Again he decided not to criticize their mutinous behavior during the preceding weeks. Instead he encouraged them to discipline themselves and to follow orders. He then left to prepare for the long journey.

Austin was dismayed by the choice of men who were to accompany him to the United States as his fellow commissioners. William Wharton had been his enemy for years, "a man I cannot act with," wrote Austin, "a man . . . destitute of political honesty, and whose attention is much more devoted to injure me than to serve the country." He had a slightly better opinion of Dr. Branch T. Archer, whom he believed had good intentions, but, Austin Said, "he is very wild." Austin knew, however, that if the people of the United States could see the three commissioners cooperating despite their differences, they would have a much better chance at successfully negotiating the $1 million in loans that Texas needed so desperately. Once again, Austin put his personal feelings aside and agreed to do his part. There was no doubt, however, that Austin considered himself the leader of the three. Secure about his own importance and people's awareness of his work in Texas, he had business cards printed for use in the United States that identified him simply as "Stephen F. Austin, of Texas."

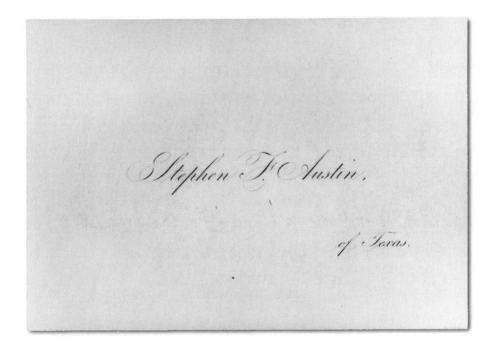

This is Stephen F. Austin's calling card. It is common belief that he had these cards printed for his diplomatic mission to the United States in 1836.

6. The Mission

Christmas of 1835 found Austin at the mouth of the Brazos River, arranging his personal affairs and preparing for what he knew would be a long and difficult trip to the United States. He was depressed, having learned that his best friend and partner Samuel May Williams had fled the United States. While attending the territorial legislature in Monclova, Mexico, Williams had gone against the Mexican government in some way Austin did not understand. Austin, Williams, and a wealthy investor, Thomas McKinney, had intended to develop a town near the mouth of the Brazos. Now, with Williams gone, the plan would have to be postponed. Leaving his interest in the matter in charge of his sister Emily's husband, James, Austin sailed for New Orleans with Wharton and Archer on December 26.

Their mission to the United States would be difficult. There was great support for Texas there, but some in the United States felt that Texas should just settle the differences with Mexico and not seek American assistance. This was because the government that

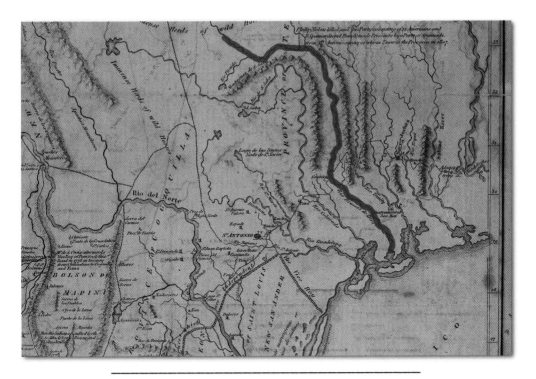

This 1807 map of New Spain was based on the sketches of Zebulon M. Pike, who traveled through the country in 1807. The Brazos River, spelled Brassos on the map, is outlined in red. Stephen F. Austin had entertained plans of developing a town near the Brazos River. However, he put them aside to travel to the United States, where he sought American funds and support for the Texans.

Texas established had not pushed to declare independence from Mexico. Of course, it was Austin who had opposed complete separation, but once he learned that Santa Anna was marching north with an army, Austin had announced his support for a declaration of independence. Texas's government council called a convention to meet on the first of March to consider it. Austin, Wharton, and Archer all agreed the convention should meet sooner. It was the first time Austin and Wharton had found themselves on the same side of an issue, and it was easier for the two of them to begin working together. Unlike many politicians, once Austin realized he had been mistaken in opposing independence, he admitted it and did everything he could to correct it.

The army that Austin left behind in San Antonio, meanwhile, had great success. Under Colonel Ben Milam, on December 5, the volunteers had finally stormed through the city. They defeated and captured Cos and his army with very few casualties.

January 6, 1836, was a high moment for Austin in the United States. For once, his health was good, and he and the other commissioners addressed a huge gathering in New Orleans. By the time they left the city to go farther north, they had promises of loans totaling $250,000, a quarter of what they had come to raise. Only a small amount of it, however, was given immediately.

When they reached Nashville, Tennessee, in early February, their mission nearly ground to a halt. Winter storms iced the roads and the rivers, Wharton and Austin both caught serious cases of the flu, and there was no more good news from Texas. In Nashville, they received enthusiastic public support but no more money, and Austin wrote home that, unless Texas declared independence and rushed documents to the commissioners giving them power to make deals for Texas as a separate country, it would be "almost useless for us to appear in Washington." Ironically, Austin wrote this on March 3, the day after Texas did indeed

This undated portrait of Colonel Benjamin Milam was created
by Charles B. Normann. Milam was killed near the beginning of the
Texas Revolution. However, Milam's leadership had inspired his
fellow Texans to retake San Antonio from Mexican forces in 1835.

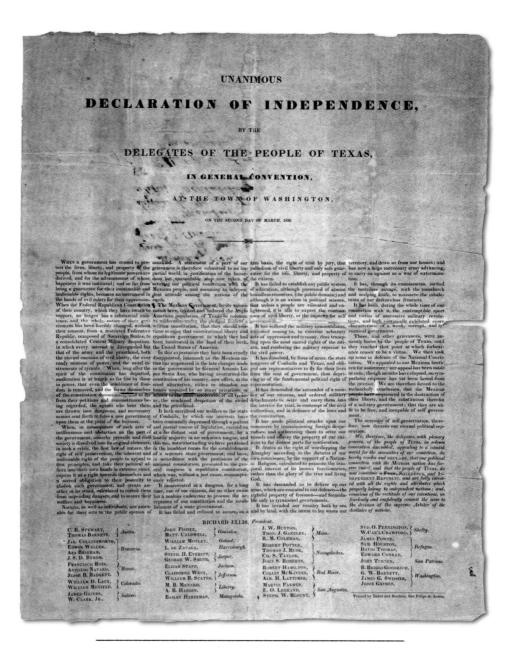

Texas's Declaration of Independence, adopted on March 2, 1836, contains statements on the function and the responsibility of government. The document concludes by declaring Texas a free and an independent republic.

declare independence, but communications with Texas were almost entirely cut off, and Austin had no way of knowing about Texas having declared independence.

On March 7, Austin addressed a large crowd in Louisville, Kentucky. The cause of Texas, he implored them for more than an hour, "is the cause of light and liberty;—the same holy cause for which our forefathers fought and bled:—the same that has an advocate in the bosom of every freeman." Again people were friendly, but Austin and the other commissioners raised little money. In Louisville, Austin crossed paths with Samuel May Williams, and they had a joyous reunion. Austin had been warned that Williams was involved in illegal land speculations, which was why Williams had fled to the United States. Austin refused to believe it.

The terrible weather had put the commissioners behind schedule. Wharton was too sick to go anywhere, and he remained in Nashville. Austin sent Archer to Cincinnati, Ohio, and he took a difficult coach ride to Lexington, Kentucky. Austin was there only one day, during which he had a happy reunion with his beloved cousin, Mary Austin Holley, and visited with friends. He left Mary a copy of a speech to publish in the hope of raising more money. However, the pledges of support he received were on the strength of his personal ties alone. No good news from Texas had arrived yet.

The Texas commissioners reunited and reached Washington, D.C., at the end of March. Word finally

came of Texas's Declaration of Independence, but it was from newspapers and gossip. The American government received no official notice from Texas, and, without it, could not give money to Austin and his colleagues. The commissioners themselves were not even sure who was in charge of Texas and addressed their letters helplessly to "The Government." As the situation was impossible, the three decided to split up. Wharton was a personal friend of President Andrew Jackson's, and Wharton stayed in Washington to watch events there. Dr. Archer traveled to Richmond, Virginia, to appeal to what the commissioners hoped would be a friendly southern audience. Austin himself made a trip through Baltimore to Philadelphia, where he tried to obtain a $500,000 loan from the Bank of the United States. The bank's president, Nicholas Biddle,

This 1799 engraving of the Bank of the United States in Philadelphia was created and published by W. Birch & Son. Horses and wagons are shown passing in front of the bank, which was located on Third Street.

Opposite: This 1839 map by David H. Burr shows the United States of America and parts of neighboring countries. Some key American cities are marked with borders. For example, New Orleans, Louisiana, is bordered by orange; Nashville, Tennessee, by yellow; and Washington, D.C., by blue.

This is a copy of Henry A. McArdle's painting of William Barret Travis. Travis (1809–1836) was one of the first to join the Texan forces when friction developed between Texas and Mexico. He commanded Texan forces against Santa Anna's Mexican army at the Alamo and was killed when Santa Anna's men stormed the fort.

turned him down. Austin went on to New York, where he arrived on April 12, and he began meeting with politicians and bankers at once.

News of the war in Texas finally began to arrive, and all the news was awful. Two of Austin's rebellious army colonels, William Barret Travis and Jim Bowie, had disobeyed Sam Houston's order, which was to destroy the San Antonio fortress known as the Alamo and then retreat. When Santa Anna entered the city, he trapped them and their men. After laying siege to the Alamo for thirteen days, Santa Anna stormed the fort and massacred more than 180 defenders. Another of Austin's disobedient officers, James Walker Fannin, was also defeated by the Mexican army. Fannin and his men were imprisoned briefly in the mission at Goliad, and then on Santa Anna's orders, he and four hundred survivors were lined up and were shot by Mexican soldiers. Sam Houston had finally managed to establish himself in command of the Texas army, but he was in full retreat even as he was trying to train and to drill them into an effective fighting force. Understandably, many people in the United States believed that Texas was finished, and it made the Texas commissioners' job to raise aid very hard.

Austin stayed in New York for three weeks pleading for assistance from whomever would meet with him,

The following spread is an 1836 map of the San Antonio–Alamo area. It was prepared by a Mexican army engineer for one of Santa Anna's generals. The map provided Santa Anna's soldiers with a view of the battlefield's hills, valleys, rivers, and other features.

Alamo.

Bejar.

Villita.

Explicacion de las partes de la Por[...]

A. Entrada.
B. Habitaciones de Ofici[...]
C. Cuerpo de guardia.
D. Cobrand.º de Artiller[...]
E. Cuartel de Yd.
F. Cuarteles.
G. Parque.
H. Foso interior.
Y. Caballero alto.
J. Bateria á barveta.
L. Yd. atroncrada.
M. Yd. id.
N. Yd. á barveta.
O. Fosos exteriores.

This photograph of an old Spanish mission at the Goliad State Historical Park was taken in 1996. The town of Goliad was an important location during the Texas Revolution. Any Mexican naval supply line to San Antonio passed by Goliad, making it a strategic location for the Texan army.

but he had no success. Angry and frustrated, he used poor judgment and published a shocking speech in which he described the Texas conflict as a race war "waged by the mongrel Spanish-Indian and Negro race, against civilization and the Anglo-American race." Austin felt he had to say something extreme to shake up the Americans. He did not really hold such hateful views. In fact back home many of his closest friends, the Navarros and the Seguíns, were Hispanic. Moreover, Austin had always been troubled by the idea of slavery.

He sacrificed his values in making this speech, and it did not even help to raise funds for Texas. Wharton joined him in New York, but, for all their labor, they managed a loan of only $100,000, and, of that, only $10,000 was paid up front. Austin left New York on May 24 for a port on the Ohio River to begin the long journey back to New Orleans.

At this time, he learned stunning news. In Texas, Santa Anna had chased Houston's little army across the whole territory, until Houston turned and crushed him in the Battle of San Jacinto on April 21. Half the Mexican army had been killed and the other half had been captured. Texas's independence was a reality, and Austin had to get home as fast as possible.

Austin learned a couple of important lessons from this long and tiring journey through the United States. The first was that, although he saw that there was enormous public sympathy for Texas's cause in the United States, the banks and the moneylenders who were in a position to help Texas win her independence were more concerned with protecting their profits than they were willing to risk money for people's freedom. This disappointed him greatly. "Had I known as much of these kind of people last winter as I do now," he

Following spread: The following spread shows the Battle of San Jacinto, which took place on April 21, 1836. Sam Houston led Texans in this charge against Santa Anna's Mexican troops. The battle for Texas was ultimately won during this conflict.

wrote in a letter, "I should not have spent any time upon them."

The second lesson was happier. He had gone to the United States with a low opinion of his companions, Wharton and Archer, but, by the time he returned to Texas, he had changed his mind. Of Wharton, whom he had considered his worst enemy, he wrote that they were "on the best of terms and I have no doubt will always continue to be—it is not any fault that we ever were otherwise . . . we [had] not known each other personally as we might and ought to have." He had once described Branch Archer as "very wild." Now he wrote that Archer "is truly a noble fellow . . . and I am very much attached to him." Austin realized that it was not wise to form harsh opinions of people he did not know well.

When Austin's boat landed in New Orleans on June 10, he learned that Santa Anna had been captured the day after the Battle of San Jacinto. Knowing that his diplomatic skills would now be needed back home, Austin stayed in New Orleans only long enough to buy a shipload of supplies for his new country before he continued home. Voyages always made him seasick, but when he landed at the mouth of the Brazos on June 27, there was no time to rest and to recover. Texas's government and army were both in great disorder.

Sam Houston had been dangerously wounded during the battle and had gone to New Orleans to have bone fragments removed from his ankle. Many in the army refused to obey orders from the new general, Mirabeau Lamar, and there was a loud clamor to execute Santa Anna, which Austin knew would horrify civilized countries and would cost Texas much goodwill. During Austin's absence, the Texas government had reorganized itself under a temporary president, David G. Burnet, who was an old friend of his. Most of he army hated Burnet, however. Austin approached Burnet with a plan, under which Santa Anna would ask the American president, Andrew Jackson, to guarantee the peace between Texas and Mexico, after which Santa Anna would be allowed to return home. Austin did not trust Santa Anna to tell the truth; what he wanted was for the United States to guarantee Texas's safety until Texas could join the other states. Austin did not view Santa Anna's unreliability as an issue in getting U.S. protection.

Santa Anna was being held in a remote plantation house to keep him out of reach of the army. When Austin met him there on July 1, the circumstances were rather different from their last meeting. Back then Austin had been destined for prison, and Santa Anna had been at the height of his powers. After much discussion between Austin and Santa Anna, the Mexican president agreed to be escorted to Washington, D.C., to meet with the American president himself. Texas was spared the shame of executing a defeated head of state.

LETTER FROM S. F. AUSTIN TO G. BORDEN, JR.

Mr. G. Borden Jr.:

Dear Sir,—I have just received your letter of the 15th instant, informing me that great efforts are making to circulate reports and slanders, for the purpose of injuring me, at the election which is to be held on the first Monday of next month. Such things are to be expected. In all communities there are men, who attempt to rise and effect their individual views, by trying to mislead the public. The check upon them, is the appeal to your mind of a few facts.

I have been connected with the public affairs of Texas, in one way or another, for fifteen years, and under circumstances, during the whole of that period, the most difficult, perplexing and embarrassing.

I was for many years the principal organ of the local administration, and of communication between the settlers of this colony, (who, be it remembered, came direct from a free and well organised government, the United States, with all their political ideas and habits fresh upon their minds,) and the Mexican government, which then was, as it still is, in that state of chaos produced by a sudden transition from extreme slavery and ignorance, to extreme republican liberty. The difficulty of such a position is evident. The dangers of premature and ruinous collisions, produced by a difference of language, forms, laws, habits, &c., were almost insurmountable. The very nature of things opened an almost boundless field for demagogues and personalities, and the country was placed, during th whole of that eventful period, upon a volcano, subject to be ruined by popular excitements on the one hand, or by the jealousy of the Mexicans on the other. I was individually liable to suspicion, and to fancied or real complaints from all quarters; and a mark for the shafts of envy, and personal animosity, as well as for the attacks of those who honestly differed in opinion with me, or were misinformed. That period was more difficult and dangerous to the settlement of Texas, and to its ultimate emancipation and liberty, than any which has subsequently threatened, or which now threatens its destinies; for had its colonization failed, there would have been no foundation to plant independence, or any thing else upon.

We passed through that period, however, in safety. A foundation was then laid, which I believed, and an now convinced, could not, and cannot be broken up. No one knows or can appreciate so well as I do, the labor it has cost, and perhaps but few have maturely considered its strength, and results—they are co-durable with the English language and with the Anglo-American race.

In April, 1833, I was appointed by the people of Texas, represented in general convention, to go to the city of Mexico as their agent or commissioner, to apply for the admission of Texas into the Mexican confederation as a State. This appointment was ruinous to my individual interests, and in every respect hazardous and fatiguing. I accepted it, however, from a sense of duty and went to Mexico at my individual expense, for I never asked, or received one dollar from the country for that trip. I was imprisoned in Mexico, as is wellknown, and detained about two years. During this time, it seems that some persons engaged in large land speculations at Monclova, the seat of government of the state of Coahuila and Texas. These are the speculations to which you allude in your letter of the 15th instant, and which, you say, are ruinous to my election.— You ask me to say whether I am or not, concerned in them.

The whole of the circumstances connected with that affair —my absence from the country at the time—the almost impossibility of communicating with me then, owing to my imprisonment in Mexico—my known, and uniform, and undeviating opposition to every thing that was in any manner calculated to entangle the land or political affairs of Texas—all, prove to impartial minds, that I was not concerned in them. But, as you ask me a direct question, I am interested or not, I say positively that I never was interested in those speculations nor do I know the full history of them, past, nor am I certain that I know the full particulars.

[text partially illegible] ... election of November last, ... month—it was the ... whether the Constitution ... the country to take, or ... with certain limitations, ... land, and as such, it ... sustain it, until it was ... principle at that time ...

seems that I am now denounced for so doing, and isolated expressions are raked up, without any reference to the peculiar circumstances and temporary excitements of those days, or to the idea which was entertained by many, of trying to keep the seat of war beyond the limits of Texas, until the country was better prepared, and by that means save the families from the devastations of invasion which they have suffered.

I was appointed, and not at my solicitation, by the said November Convention, to go to the United States as a Commissioner in conjunction with Dr. B. T. Archer, and W. H. Wharton, Esq. I obeyed the call of my country, thus expressed, and labored faithfully and arduously in the cause, as did both of my colleagues. Our services were of a nature that it is difficult to explain or appreciate—we made loans that were beneficial, and did not hesitate to pledge our private property— our accounts have been rendered to the government and are matter of record—we labored assiduously to enlighten and inform the public mind, as to the origin, principles, and objects of the contest with Mexico, and in every respect obeyed our instructions. The estimate in which my own services were held by my colleagues is sufficiently shown by their request that I would be a candidate for President, and by their support of my election. And yet it is now charged upon me as a sort of crime that I obeyed the call of the November Convention, and left Texas at all, and it is also said that nothing was done by the Commissioners but to eat fine dinners, drink wine, &c.

Such is the kind of slang you inform me will destroy my election. The people ought to be competent to analize these matters, and judge for themselves. They are however liable to be misled, by wrong impressions, but will do justice in the end, and I assure you that it will be no personal mortification to me, individually, if I am not elected while such erroneous impressions exist. I have one proud consolation which nothing can deprive me of, and that is the approbation of my own conscience, and the certainty that all I have done since I came to Texas in 1821, will bear the test of the most rigid scrutiny. I do not pretend by this to say, that I have not erred in judgment, and perhaps from imprudent council, but I do say, that no man has labored with purer intentions, or with a more ardent and disinterested desire to promote the prosperity, and happiness, and liberty of Texas, and I also say, that I consented to become a candidate at this election with great reluctance. I have been absent from Texas, on public business, for about three years. During this time, my individual affairs have been neglected, and much of the old colonizing business remained unclosed. It was my wish and intention to devote this year to those objects, at the same time giving all the aid I could, as a citizen, to the public cause.

You requested a reply to your letter—I have given a long one, and you can make any use of it you think proper.

Respectfully, your fellow citizen,

S. F. AUSTIN.

Printed at the Office of the "TELEGRAPH," Columbia, Texas.

This is a transcript of Austin's letter to Gail Borden Jr. about the election for Texas's first president. In this letter, Austin writes that he received Borden's warning that people were spreading lies to keep Austin from becoming president. Borden was the official surveyor in Austin's Texas colony. A surveyor judges the quality of land and sets a price on it.

The government under Burnet was just a temporary one. The election of a permanent government was scheduled for September 1836. Archer and Wharton were now back from the United States, and Austin met them in the town of Velasco, Texas, so they could prepare a report of their trip. When they met, Archer, Wharton, and several other leading citizens asked Austin to run for president of Texas. Stephen F. Austin was a modest man, but there is no doubt that he believed he was the man best qualified to lead the new country. In these years, a person could not just announce that he was running for president. It was important to appear to be summoned by the masses. On August 4, Austin issued a statement, using language that was very stiff and formal:

"I have been nominated by many persons, whose opinions I am bound to respect, as a candidate for the office of President of Texas, at the September elections.

"Influenced by the governing principle which has regulated my actions since I came to Texas, fifteen years ago, which is to serve the country in any capacity in which the people might think proper to employ me, I shall not decline the highly responsible and difficult one now proposed, should the majority of my fellow citizens elect me."

7. The Idol of My Existence

During the campaign for president of Texas, Austin quickly realized how unpopular he had become. Many Texans resented him for remaining friendly to Mexico as long as he had. Others blamed him for a land scandal of which he was, in fact, completely innocent. Still others held him responsible for saving Santa Anna's life, even though in the heat of the campaign Austin lied and blamed that on his main opponent, Sam Houston. In fact both men worked to keep Santa Anna alive. In any event, Austin could read the public's mood well enough to know he had no chance of being elected.

Texas's first presidential balloting was held on September 5, 1836. It took several days for returns to come in from remote areas, but it quickly became clear that Austin had been humiliated. Sam Houston won with more than five thousand votes, nearly ten times as many votes as Austin had. Even a third man, who pulled out of the race, received more votes than Austin. The election left Austin hurt, bitter, and angry. He had created Texas out of raw wilderness. It had taken

This is the Texas flag and seal design,
created by Peter Krag. The design for the flag
and the seal were approved on January 25, 1839.

fifteen years of his life and had broken his health, where-
as Sam Houston had done nothing for Texas but win the
war, and now Houston was to be rewarded with the pres-
idency. "A successful military chieftain is hailed with
admiration and applause," Austin wrote sarcastically to
his cousin Mary, "but the bloodless pioneer of the wilderness, like the corn and cotton he causes to spring where it
never grew before, attracts no notice. . . . No slaughtered
thousands or smoking cities attest his devotion to the
cause of human happiness, and he is regarded by the

mass of the world as a humble instrument to pave the way for others."

Sam Houston knew that Austin deserved to win and admitted it in his first speech as president. Houston also knew, however, that Austin had become so unpopular that he would have found it impossible to run the country. Losing the election had so upset Austin that he became sicker than ever before, but Houston still needed his help. The two men agreed that Texas's first major goal was to be annexed, or joined, to the United States, which would put Texas under the protection of the U.S. government, and Houston understood that Austin could help bring this about. Austin's name carried more weight in the United States than did anyone else's; he remained the most experienced diplomat in Texas. Rather than let Austin disappear into private life, Houston offered him a job as secretary of state. He knew Austin was sick, but, in those days, when it took weeks just for a letter to cross the country, the job would not tire him. His daily duties would be fewer because correspondence between him and other officials would travel slowly.

Contributing to Austin's illness during this time was the emotional strain of a terrible quarrel he had had with his longtime best friend and secretary, Samuel May Williams. Austin never married or started a family of his own. In substitution, he assumed a lot of responsibility for his nieces and nephews. He also formed friendships that were more emotional than was common for men in his time, such as his relationship with Williams. Sadly, Austin was a better friend to Williams than Williams was to him. During the previous year, Williams had gone to the state capital at Monclova and used his friendship with the great Austin to influence the legislature into making shady and treacherous land deals. Williams stood to make a fortune by these land deals, though ruining Austin's reputation for open and honest business in the process. Rumors of Williams's misbehavior had reached Austin before the presidential campaign. They surfaced again when Austin ran for president, making him look bad, so he blamed Williams for his defeat. Of course, he would have lost anyway, but Austin was heartbroken about the betrayal. When the Mexican government learned of Williams's dealings, Williams was forced to flee into hiding in the United States. "Sam Williams," Austin now wrote him, "you were wound around and rooted in my affections more than any man ever was or ever can be again. . . . You must have known that the odium of all . . . those Monclova matters . . . were morally wrong, and they have some very criminal and dreadful features."

Williams insisted that he had done nothing wrong. "No matter what you believe toward me," he wrote back, "and no matter what I may suffer — greater is my esteem for you . . . long ago have I sworn eternal friendship."

Austin was now faced with the decision of whether to make a friend take responsibility for his actions or to forgive him and take him back. Williams's guilt was beyond doubt, but Austin was too sick and lonely to do without his best friend. "I read your letter with such feelings," Austin replied, "as a drowning man would seize a plank. . . . You have greatly vexed and worried and distressed me, [but] my anger is becoming almost exhausted. . . . Williams you have wounded me very deeply, but you are so deeply rooted in my affections, that with all your faults, you are at heart too much like a wild and heedless brother to be entirely banished. Come home."

Austin could have continued to mope around Peach Point and to feel sorry for himself, but he didn't. Texas, he wrote a friend, had become "the idol of my existence." He had helped to create a huge new country, and when President Houston asked him to be secretary of state, he could not refuse the call for help. Despite his poor health, Austin journeyed from Peach Point to the capital, which had been moved to Columbia, and was luckily only a few miles (km) up the Brazos River.

As secretary of state, one of his first tasks was to arrange for the transfer of prisoners of war (POWs) with Texas's former enemy, Mexico. For most of the POWs, this was quickly arranged, but the most important prisoner was Santa Anna himself, the dictator of Mexico, who had been captured just after the Battle of San Jacinto. Because of his shocking massacres at the Alamo and Goliad, many important Texans, including a majority of the Senate, were calling for his trial and execution. Houston and Austin agreed, however, that Santa Anna was worth much more to them alive. To kill the leader of a defeated country would set a bad example for Texas to begin her life as a nation. Now, as secretary of state, Austin completed the arrangements he had started before the presidential campaign to get the dictator out of the country. Austin sent him on a trip to the United States, where Santa Anna agreed to recognize Texas in talks with the American president, Andrew Jackson.

The same day that Houston was elected president, Texas citizens voted overwhelmingly to seek annexation to the United States, and, because nearly all Texans had once been Americans, they assumed that this would be easy to accomplish. In the United States, however, Texas represented a thorny political problem. The northern and southern states had been quarreling ever more bitterly about the right of the southern states to allow slavery. To keep the country together, the Senate was carefully balanced with an equal number of free states and slave states. Texas would enter the country as a slave state. This would tip the Senate balance in favor of the South, and powerful northern senators were strongly against this unbalance. As much as President Jackson wanted to add Texas to the Union, he was powerless to make it happen. Austin's most important task as Texas's secretary of state was doomed to failure.

This portrait of Andrew "Old Hickory" Jackson was painted by Ralph Eleaser Whiteside Earl. Andrew Jackson, who lived from 1767 to 1845, was the seventh president of the United States. His method of trying to appeal to the majority of voters has become known as Jacksonian democracy.

There was very little money in the frontier republic. As Austin took stock of his personal situation, he recognized that he did not have even a roof to cover his head. His own house in San Felipe had been burned during the war, and he lived during this time in two rooms in the family compound at Peach Point. In Columbia, he stayed in a rented cabin next door to the capitol building and complained bitterly of his situation in letters to friends and family.

As former empresario, Austin still owned vast amounts of land on which he could support himself, but he also felt great responsibility for those of his family when he had previously encouraged to settle in Texas. Instead of providing for his own comfort, he sold $3,000 worth of land to help his sister, Emily, get back to the United States. She had wanted to flee from the war, but Austin had insisted she stay in Texas and share the fate of the country. Now that her health was failing, he wanted to put her within reach of good doctors and in a place where she could get a good education for her children. He should have taken better care of himself as well.

In mid-December, a frigid cold front blew through Columbia. In Texas, these are known as blue northers, and they can turn warm, balmy weather into an icy blast within a few hours. Austin caught a cold, which his body was too worn down to resist. He took to bed, but the rude cabin in which he stayed offered little shelter. "The little room where the bed was," according to

This stone marks the spot where George B. McKinstry's home once stood. The stone was erected by the state of Texas in 1936. McKinstry (1802–1837) was a member of Stephen F. Austin's Texas colony and a soldier in the Battle of Velasco. Austin died in McKinstry's house on December 27, 1836.

one visitor, had "open clap board walls and no fireplace or stove. . . . It turned very cold." The day after Christmas, a few doctors were called in. They discovered that Austin's cold had turned into a bad case of pneumonia. They decided to give him an emetic to make him vomit, hoping that it would help him to breathe better. Austin did seem to get better. At night, he was able, at times, to sit up at a table where he could breathe easier, but he was too weak to sit up for long. At nine in the morning of December 27, 1836, he was given additional treatment, which seemed to help a bit, and he whispered, "Now I will go to sleep." Over the next two hours, he woke a few times and had some tea. He was tended by his brother-in-law, by his nephew, Dr. Archer, and also by the French doctor Theodore Leger.

During his fever, Austin dreamed that the United States had agreed that Texas was a separate country. Delirious, Austin rose up from his sweaty pallet shortly before noon. "The independence of Texas is recognized!" he exclaimed. "Don't you see it in the papers? Doctor Archer told me so." Stephen F. Austin, age forty-three, died half an hour later; it was December 27, 1836. President Sam Houston issued a sad proclamation almost immediately. "The Father of

This portrait of Stephen F. Austin, done near the end of his life, was probably painted for Henry Austin or Mary Austin Holley. The image later appeared on Republic of Texas fifty-dollar bills.

THE PATRIARCH HAS LEFT US.

WE perform a most painful duty in announcing the death of GENERAL STEPHEN F. AUSTIN, *who departed this life, yesterday, at half-past* 12 *o'clock,* P. M. *at the house of judge McKinstry. His friends and relations have sustained an irreparable loss; his country, just merging into existence, the best and tenderest of fathers; the sons and daughters of Texas have now full cause for mourning, with one solitary consolation, that they will meet the just man above.*

His remains will leave for Peach Point, for interment, at twelve o'clock to-day.

Columbia, December 28, 1836.

P. S. The steamboat having arrived, the remains of General Austin will be removed from judge McKinstry's at eight o'clock to-morrow morning, to the steamboat, at Columbia Landing, and not to-day, as above stated.

This is the funeral notice for Stephen F. Austin, which was printed by his friend Gail Borden Jr. Borden believed that Austin deserved to be recognized as a martyr who had sacrificed his interests, health, and life for Texas.

Texas is no more!" it read. "The first pioneer of the wilderness has departed!"

News of Stephen F. Austin's passing plunged Texas into grief, as the people gave him in death the recognition that they had been unwilling to give him while he was alive. At President Houston's order, cannons thundered from Texas's frontier forts in twenty-three-gun salutes, one for each county in the nation. All government officials began wearing black armbands for thirty days of official mourning, as Houston and an honor guard accompanied the "Great Empresario's" body aboard the steamboat *Yellow Stone* to the family

The depiction of the steamboat *Yellow Stone* is based on a painting by Karl Bodmer. Once the steamboat reached Peach Point, Stephen F. Austin's body was laid to rest.

This statue marks the grave of Stephen F. Austin. He died at just forty-three years old, but he lived long enough to see a part of his dream realized. Texas had been converted from a wilderness into a land settled by ambitious colonists.

compound at Peach Point, where he was buried on December 29.

Few men in history can claim an accomplishment the equal of Stephen F. Austin's. In fifteen years of dedicated labor, he established civilization in a huge and raw wilderness and played his part in creating a proud and an important nation. Texas would have to remain independent for nearly ten more years before the United States was forced to accept her as a state, but once this was done, Austin's reputation as a great American was secured.

Timeline

1793   Stephen F. Austin is born in Austinville, Virginia, on November 3.

1819   National financial panic ruins the Austin family's finances.

1812–1818   Stephen serves in the Missouri territorial legislature.

1821   Moses Austin dies on June 10.

1821   In December, the first American colonists begin arriving in Texas.

1822   The Spanish government is overthrown. The new Mexican government refuses to recognize Stephen Austin's colony.

            In April, Austin receives a new colonization contract from the Mexican congress to settle three hundred families.

1830   The Ley of April 6 forbids further American immigration into Texas.

1832   The Anáhuac Disturbances take place.

1833   The Convention of 1833 renews petitions

for governmental reforms, including Mexican statehood for Texas, separate from Coahuila. Austin is sent to present the petitions to central government.

1834   Austin is arrested at Saltillo for suspicion of inciting revolt. He is brought back to Mexico City and held there.

In December, Austin is released on bail but is forced to remain in Mexico City.

1835   In July, Austin is freed by general amnesty. He returns to Texas via New Orleans at the end of August.

On September 8, Austin gives his approval for a Consultation of the people to convene and to consider what to do about Mexican rule.

On October 2, the Texas Revolution begins at Gonzales.

On November 8, Austin asks to be relieved as commander of the volunteer army.

On November 12, Austin is named commissioner to the United States to seek support for the Texas Revolution.

On November 23, Austin orders his army to assault San Antonio. The army refuses. Austin announces his departure to the troops the following day.

On December 26, Austin, with William Harris Wharton and Branch Archer, sail for the United States as commissioners.

1836   On January 6, Austin addresses a large public meeting in New Orleans and successfully negotiates a loan of $250,000.

On August 4, Austin announces his candidacy for president of the Republic of Texas.

On September 5, Austin is defeated overwhelmingly for president.

On October 28, Austin is confirmed as secretary of state.

On December 27, Austin dies at Columbia. Texas begins thirty days of official mourning.

Glossary

Anáhuac Disturbances (ah-NAH-wok dih-STER-bin-sez) In Texas in 1832, a series of clashes between American colonists and Mexican authorities that nearly began the Texas Revolution then instead of three years later.

annexation (a-nek-SAY-shun) To add or to join one piece of territory to another, as the United States annexed Texas in 1845.

badgered (BA-jurd) Bothered; pestered.

black marketeer (BLAK mar-kih-TEER) One who trades in goods that are outlawed.

boorish (BOOR-ish) Having bad or rude manners.

casualties (KA-zhul-teez) The toll of those killed and wounded in a battle.

centralist (SEN-truh-list) One who believes that government power ought to be concentrated in one place.

compound (KOM-pownd) A group of houses or apartments where related families live close to one another.

Consultation (kon-sul-TAY-shun) 1. In Texas, the

meeting that was held held in October 1835 to discuss what to do about problems with Mexico. 2. The name of the provisional, or temporary, government in Texas from November 15, 1835, until March 1, 1836.

delegates (DEH-lih-gets) Representatives elected to attend a political gathering.

destitute (DES-tih-toot) Very poor; penniless.

dictator (DIK-tay-ter) One who exercises supreme authority in a country, usually without having been elected to do so.

dragoons (druh-GOONZ) Heavily armed cavalry troops.

emetic (ih-MEH-tik) Medicine to help one vomit.

empresario (em-pruh-SEHR-ee-oh) A general manager with broad powers and responsibilities.

faction (FAK-shun) One political group that is in disagreement with another.

federalist (FEH-duh-ruh-list) One who believes in a strong central government.

fret (FREHT) Worry.

frontier (frun-TEER) The far edge of a country, where people are just beginning to settle.

Hispanicized (his-PA-nih-syzd) To have adopted the

forms and customs of Hispanic culture, such as by having changed one's name from George to Jorge.

labor (LAY-ber) A Spanish unit of land measurement. A labor equals 177 acres (71 ha).

league (LEEG) A Spanish unit of land measurement. A league equals 4,428 acres (1,771 ha).

ley (LAY) A Spanish word meaning a law or statute, as the Ley of April 6, 1830, which forbade any more colonists from entering Texas from the United States.

mutinous (MYOO-tin-us) Unruly or rebellious.

odium (OH-dee-um) Dishonor, disapproval, or the state of being hated.

pneumonia (nuh-MOH-nyuh) A disease in which the lungs become inflamed and filled with thick fluid.

province (PRAH-vins) A political unit less important than a state.

resolutions (reh-zuh-LOO-shunz) The formal expression of the opinion of an assembly, voted on and adopted.

sedition (sih-DIH-shun) To cause others to rebel against the government.

smelters (SMEL-terz) Workers who refine ore to obtain metal.

squatters (SKWAH-terz) Those who settle on property

without right or title or payment of rent, and who believe that if they stay there long enough, they gain some legal claim to the land.

tracts (TRAKTS) Acreages or parcels of land not precisely measured.

treacherous (TREH-chuh-rus) False, faithless, dangerous.

treason (TREE-zun) The crime of trying to overthrow the government.

venture (VEN-chur) An undertaking that involves risk or danger.

wit (WIT) A funny and clever person.

Additional Resources

To learn more about Stephen F. Austin, check out the following books and Web sites.

Books

Barker, Eugene C. *The Father of Texas: A Life of Stephen F. Austin for Young People*. Indianapolis and New York: The Bobbs-Merrill Company, 1935.

Cantrell, Gregg. *Stephen F. Austin, Empresario of Texas*. New Haven and London: Yale University Press, 1999.

Flynn, Jean. *Stephen F. Austin, the Father of Texas, Stories for Young Americans*. Austin, Texas: Eakin Publications, 1981.

Web Sites

Due to the changing nature of Internet links, PowerPlus Books has developed an online list of Web sites related to the subject of this book. This site is updated regularly. Please use this link to access the list: www.powerkidslinks.com/lalt/austin

Bibliography

Austin, Moses. *The Austin Papers*. edited by Eugene C. Barker. Washington: American Historical Association, 1919 (vol. 1), 1928 (vol. 2); Austin, Texas: University of Texas Press, no date (vol. 3).

Barker, Eugene C. *The Father of Texas: A Life of Stephen F. Austin for Young People*. Indianapolis and New York: The Bobbs-Merrill Company, 1935.

—-. *The Life of Stephen F. Austin, Founder of Texas, 1793–1836*. Austin, Texas: Texas State Historical Association, 1949.

Cantrell, Gregg. *Stephen F. Austin, Empresario of Texas*. New Haven and London: Yale University Press, 1999.

Hammeken, George L. "Recollections of Stephen F. Austin." *Southwestern Historical Quarterly*, Vol. 20 (1916).

Holley, Mary Austin. *Texas*. Lexington, Kentucky: J. Clarke & Co., 1836.

Jones, Marie Beth. *Peach Point Plantation: The First 150 Years*. Waco, Texas: Texian Press, 1982.

Long, Walter E. *Stephen F. Austin's Legacies*. Austin, Texas: Steck-Vaughn Company, 1970.

Index

About the Author

James L. Haley is a writer who lives in Austin, Texas. He is the author of several books about Texas's history. His nonfiction works include *Sam Houston; Texas: From Spindletop to World War II; Most Excellent Sir: Letters Received by Sam Houston, President of the Republic of Texas, at Columbia, 1836-1837; Texas: An Album of History; Apaches: A History and Culture Portrait;* and *The Buffalo War: A History of the Red River Indian Uprising of 1874.*

Credits

Photo Credits

Cover: courtesy, Texas State Library and Archives Commission (portrait); Library of Congress Geography and Map Division Washington, D.C. (map). Pp. 4, 15, 30, 49, 67, 72 Library of Congress Geography and Map Division Washington, D.C.; pp. 6, 8, 21, 24, 55, 58, 69, 74, 80–81, 87 courtesy, Texas State Library and Archives Commission; pp. 9, 25, 41, Center for American History, University of Texas at Austin; p. 12 courtesy, Texas Memorial Museum, (Item 750–4); pp. 18, 92 © Bettmann/CORBIS; pp. 26, 39, Prints & Photographs Collection, Center for American History, University of Texas at Austin; p. 27 Daughters of the Republic of Texas Library; p. 33 Texas General Land Office; pp. 35, 84 courtesy of Rare Books & Manuscripts Collection New York Public Library Astor, Lenox, and Tilden Foundations; p. 36 Dallas Historical Society; p. 38 photo courtesy of Edward E. Ayer Collection, the Newberry Library, Chicago; p. 42 Rosenberg Library, Galveston, Texas; p. 45 © SuperStock; p. 47 East Texas Research Center, Stephen F. Austin State University; p. 51 The San Jacinto Museum of History, Houston; p. 52 Prints & Photographs Collection, James Perry Bryan Collection, Center for American History, University of Texas at Austin; p. 63 Austin (Stephen Fuller) Papers, Center for American History, University of Texas at Austin; p. 65 Perry (Hally Ballinger Bryan) Papers, Center for American History, University of Texas at Austin; pp. 70, 96 Broadsides Collection, Earl Vandale Collection, Center for American History University of Texas at Austin; p. 73 Independence National Historical Park; pp. 76–77 Map Collection, Center for American History, University of Texas at Austin; p. 78 © Danny Lehman/CORBIS; p. 94 Brazoria County Historical Museum, Angleton, Texas; p. 95 Texas State Library & Archives Commission; p. 97 © Historical Picture Archive/CORBIS; p. 98 © Dallas Hoppestad.

Editor
Leslie Kaplan

Series Design
Laura Murawski

Layout Design
Corinne Jacob

Photo Researcher
Jeffrey Wendt